About Us

For as long as I can remember dogs have been one of the most important relationships in my life; as I child I spent hours reading, researching, learning about anything 'dog'. I was passionate and absolutely devoted.

When I met Steve, he encouraged that love, and supported my passion, helping to create the life we have now alongside the dogs. We have owned and bred Leavitt Bulldogs for 13 years, and they are a huge part of our family. Our life is shaped around them and their needs.

I am on the Leavitt Bulldog Association Board of Directors and after having been selected by David Leavitt to help preserve the breed, I am also the breed representative for the U.K. I take the responsibly of protecting the breed very seriously, not just the bloodline, but the future of the puppies we breed. I believe the success of a breeder is not about show titles, dogs that fit a perfect breed standard or how many dogs you can breed. For me, success is measured on the happiness and quality of life for each dog, living with their families until their last days. This happiness is only achievable with ongoing support, advice and care. The placement of puppies is crucial and matching the correct families with each individual puppy is key in ensuring they go to homes that last them a lifetime. A breeder's role is not about producing puppies, but being responsible for them for as long as needed.

Our love affair with bulldogs began with our first Bulldog Bert about 14 years ago - he was not a Leavitt Bulldog and no relation to the blood line, but was a similar type in appearance. Unfortunately, aged 3 he had to be put to sleep, as he suffered with chronic allergies and his life became so.uncomfortable. He couldn't be cured and we were left with little option.

Living alongside this suffering and heartbreak made us realise that although on the surface a dog may look healthier, in reality the breeding that goes on behind the creation of these modern bulldogs (and many other breeds) isn't always done particularly well or with health in mind.

With the health issues that Bert suffered with fresh in our minds, we wanted to do as much research that we could to avoid these problems for our next dog. When we came across the Leavitt Bulldog, we were impressed with the stringent health screening that goes on within the breed. We soon decided that we were going to bring the breed to the UK, and the rest, as they say, is history - our first Leavitt Bulldogs, Billy and Rosa, were imported in 2007 from Holland and nearly 12 years on we are even more dedicated to the breed and its future.

Introduction

The purpose of this guide is primarily to help support the families that are bringing one of our puppies home; I have written this to help them get set up, and give them guidance, advice and tips on raising their new puppy. However, this advice is not just limited to the dogs I have bred, but will be of use to anyone bringing a new puppy into their home. I have spent the last 10 years tweaking everything in this book with every family along the way and as each litter grows and develops. I have used all the feedback I received from them and worked with everyone in the hope that this is the most useful advice I can provide. The simple aim of this book is to make the transition from our home to to theirs as seamless as possible for both puppy and owners!

Over the last 12 years I have spent countless hours raising puppies and young dogs, watching, learning, training and loving them. As well as breeding and raising my own puppies, I have also bought puppies into our family from other breeders at varying ages, I have also fostered a number of puppies through rescue charities.

I think it is important I am really clear, that despite all this hands on experience I am not a professional dog trainer or behaviourist, nor am I claiming to be. However, both myself and my family's life revolves around all 9 of our bulldogs and the litters we raise, as well as the families we support to raise their pups.
I have seen first hand what works, and more importantly, what does not. I am not afraid to admit I have made some mistakes along the way too and have learnt from them fast. I hope to share all of this with you in the hope you can raise your pup to be best dog they can be.

The raising of our puppies and dogs is very much a family affair - the dogs and our children need to live harmoniously for it to be a success. This is achievable with structure, respect and love. I hope I can share how I do this, what works, what doesn't. Simple and effective ways to make raising a dog a happy experience.

I will start from the very beginning by explaining what we do here in our home to get your puppy off to the best start, advise on how to prepare for arrival, puppy proofing and equipment, diet and nutrition, finding a good trainer, exercise throughout the different life stages and share general tips that I think will help you.
I also have a very unique, and friendly community surrounding the breed, made up of owners of the dogs I have bred over the years.

The Ground Work

Before your puppy is even born I am setting down the ground work to ensure everything in my power is done to ensure your puppy will become the dog you have been dreaming of, and most importantly that both the puppy and their mother are the happiest and most relaxed dogs possible.

I have carefully matched the parents of your puppy in every way possible,
starting with thorough health tests, study of conformation and most importantly good stable and friendly temperaments. I have your pup's grandparents, great grandparents, aunties and uncles all living here with our family. They live in our home, under our feet and on our sofas! So we know them inside out... You will have met them all I am sure, and got a good feel for them too. This attention to detail, combined with the correct environment for the Leavitt Bulldog, makes for a super family member, but not without the challenges along the way!

From the moment the breeding is completed I begin supporting the mother with an exceptional raw diet and supplements that will aid the growth and development of the puppy and Mum. I supplement with Folic Acid, Ester C and flax oil to help the development of bones, brain and ligaments, Sea kelp is added to support the immune system and skin. I do all I can to give everyone, Mum and Puppy, the best support possible.

The whelping box environment is crucial; the pups are born in our dining room, in the centre of our home in a peaceful, safe place that will help ensure Mum is relaxed and content. I give her 24 hour assistance, hand feeding her, help with positioning puppies with big litters, comforting and encouraging her. This helps everyone tremendously, happy puppies start in the whelping box! A calm, relaxed and happy mum makes for calm, relaxed and happy puppies.

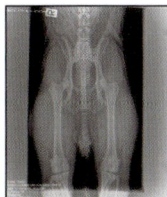

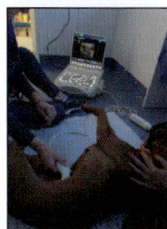

Both us and most importantly our children are present in the whelping box area as much as possible: handling, touching and interacting with the puppies and with the mother.

This early interaction is vital for the puppies' development, as this stage is when the early connections in the puppies brains are made. These connections have a bearing on their overall temperament. Dogs communicate on a whole other level to us, when they are born they can't see, or hear, but they can smell and are instinctively tuned in to subtle changes in energy from their mother. It is completely instinctive to them to communicate in this way.

To explain in more detail: when any member of our family member enters the room the puppies can smell us, they also are very in tune and sense their mothers 'energy' to our presence. If she was to react in a negative, fearful or aggressive way towards us, it's likely the puppies will sense this and they will associate our smell with her reaction. There is a chance that this initial experience remain with them – training and socialisation may break it, but the fundamental initial human contact could be negative.

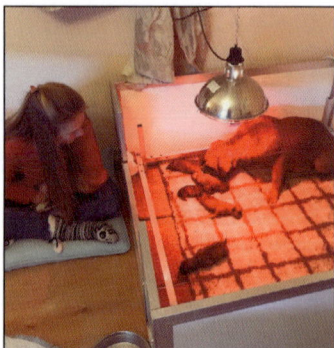

This is why the temperament of the mother dog is so important when choosing a puppy to be a family pet.

We have seen first hand how temperament is passed down from one generation to the next in our dogs and the dogs we have bred that come back to stay. We have noticed that is not just our daughter that they associate happiness and comfort with, it is any child, they are all naturally & instinctively drawn to children.

Puppy Culture

We implement a groundbreaking training and early socialisation programme called 'Puppy Culture' created by a wonderful breeder/trainer and dog expert Jane Killion.

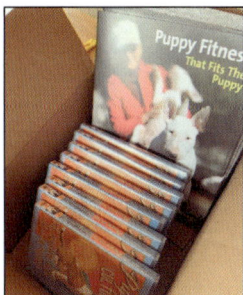

Jane developed this program with a number of professional, scientists and trainers, the aim being to shape puppies during their most influential period of development This crucial stage lasts for the first 12 weeks of their lives.

We follow her methods passionately because the results are fantastic! this is combined this with some of our own testing and socialisation methods and we couldn't be happier with how the puppies are when they leave us at 10 weeks old: well adjusted, mentally prepared, social, confident and prepared to continue training where we have left off.

I will have given you the full 'Puppy Culture' DVD along with this book - it is imperative you watch it from start to finish. I can not stress this enough.

Not only can you follow the progress we make with your puppy; most importantly you will gain the understanding of why each exercise is important, and how you can continue the program when your pup comes home.

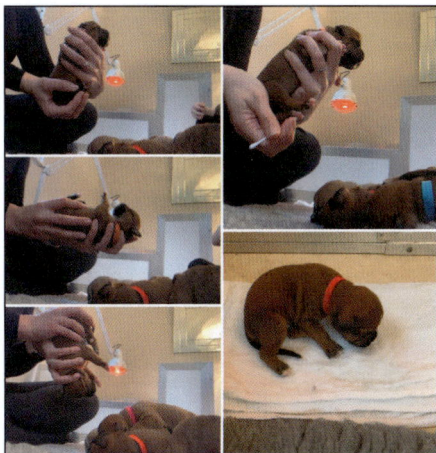

Crucially, you will have the understanding to communicate with your puppy.

During the 10 weeks your puppy is here, we cover many aspects including communication, bite inhibition, crate training, house training and resource guarding. These are all very crucial aspects of a puppy's development.

When the puppies leave us at 10 weeks the DVD will talk though the importance of continuing the last 2 weeks of the programme at home. I will go into further detail on this in the 'home time' chapter.

Getting to grips with the Puppy Culture programme will be one of the most important part of your puppy's upbringing. Getting yourself and your family familiar with what we are doing and how best to communicate with your puppy will stand you in good stead with the rest of the puppy raising to come.

Getting Everything Ready

Bringing a new puppy home is very exciting, there is so much to think about. You have your home to prepare, not to mention all the dog stuff available to buy from pet shops and online. It can be daunting and easy to get drawn into buying unnecessary or unsuitable items. I will help guide you through some of things that I have found are great, and others to stay away from.

You receive a 'puppy pack' on collection day. Included in that pack are handy things to get your pup settled; these are mainly familiar items from our home, such as bedding with a familiar smell of mum and litter mates, favourite toys and chews that they will have played with here,

along with some treats that we have been training with. The first few days of a new home can be unsettling so these things really help reassure your pup and get them comfortable quickly.

You will also have all your paperwork, insurance, vaccinations and puppy contact, along with some of my recommended toys, chews, treats and a week's worth of food.

Puppy Proofing Your Home

Your puppy is used to being in and out of our house all day and following our rules, but this does not mean they have learnt to not chew things up and get up to mischief!

Chewing is a completely normal and a healthy part of puppy development, as frustrating as it is to us! If they are chewing and exploring then they are happy and content - the key to combat disaster when it comes to chewing is you controlling what they can chew! A puppy explores the world using its mouth, they will pick up everything and anything they come across. Obvious dangers like cables, climbing up onto high furniture etc is avoidable with a little common sense. Although I do appreciate it's easier said than done at times!

My number one rule with chewing is prevention is better than cure: if you can not watch them, they should be in their pen until they are at the stage where they can be trusted alone in certain rooms. It might seem a long way off, but it will happen one day!

When they do chew items you don't want them to, don't be frustrated. This is a great opportunity to teach them its not acceptable - give them a firm verbal correction such as "NO" or "EHHH" - what ever works for you. Then introduce their toys as alternatives.

In our house we do not massively adjust anything in regards to chewing or puppy proofing, as the dogs need to learn what they can touch and play with and what they can't. Over the years we have adapted the house to be fairly dog proof but it is worth remembering that by removing everything it is very hard for them to learn what is acceptable and what is not. However we do keep everything tidy! Well, as much as possible with 9 dogs and 2 kids and if we can not watch them they are put in a safe, secure area.

Shoes and other items left on the floor are fair game for a puppy. My kids know if it is left lying around chances are it will be picked up and chewed! This does have its advantages, and is a great way to get everyone involved in keeping the house tidy. From a safety point of view, a pup chewing things other than toys and chews is dangerous , especially if it swallowed. So again, being vigilant is the best defence against the chewing stage.

Creating Boundaries

Deciding if you will allow your pup up stairs is very important, and something to be agreed on as a family, especially in the early stages.

If you do not want your dog upstairs it's worth investing in a baby gate for the bottom of the stairs. It simply prevents them going up there even when you are not watching. You will be surprised how much enjoyment a pup can't get from being chased up the stairs when they shouldn't be going up there. Before you know it it becomes a source of great entrainment to them, watching you leaping up to stop them, the ultimate game of catch!

If you are by a busy road its also worth getting some kind of gate across the front door if you don't have a garden gate etc. A puppy bolting out the door is recipe for disaster. Gates make great clear boundaries for dogs and keep them safe, especially when they are young.

These boundaries will play an important part in the first few weeks at home. they will set out in your pup's mind where they fit into the home and they will adjust accordingly. In addition to the safety aspect, boundaries will help a pup feel secure and create a layout of their home in their head.

Two of the best tools to achieve this is are a **crate and a puppy pen**. These two items may be the most important pieces of equipment I recommend to you. I suggest an adjustable pen like the one you have seen at our home. They are fairly lightweight and easy to assemble and move around. They are also worth their weight in gold! The pen can adjusted to fit any space, used in the garden, or to divide rooms etc. You can buy them online; I got ours from Amazon and have also combined two together.

Having the pen setup enables you have the puppy contained without them being shut in crate completely, providing a nice clear safe area of their own without them being too contained or restricted. It is particularly helpful if you have children or other dogs in a busy home. I know what it is like when you are making dinner for example, you are distracted from watching the kids and dogs. No one can watch their puppy every second so this is key to preserving everyone's sanity. This set up removes the stress completely, with everyone knowing the puppy is secure, relaxed and safe in their pen.

The pen is also a useful tool if the puppy reaches the deadly 'over tired stage' which happens regularly in the early stages. I find they become their most 'bitey' at this point so it is an ideal time to go to the pen with a chew or a kong to relax and encourage them to wind down .

The pen comes into play beautifully too when visitors come, as it is a great area for the pup be in when guests first arrive, and everyone is excited. Only when the puppy (and visitors) are calm can they be let out to interact in a positive and controlled way.

The are endless examples of when the pen will be useful, but the main objective is to reinforce boundaries, and offer security for your pup. Life is busy, and having a new puppy is hard at times, but this simple set up without any doubt reduces the complications and makes the whole atmosphere a more positive one.

When it comes to buying a crate to set up inside your pen you have two options:

1- Start off with a smaller one and buy a large one when they grow bigger - minimum 32 inches.

2 - Buy a full size crate they can grow into - our guys have crates they sleep in at night and are fed in and they are 48 inches. This is particularly big. A 38-42 inch crate would be more than sufficient.

It is absolutely up to you what you prefer to do.

Your puppy will have been crate trained here - they know the crate is a positive and happy place to be and will be more than happy being in there when required.

In fact they often take themselves off into their crates to sleep.

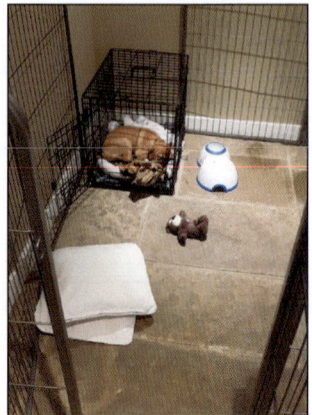

Toys and Chews

It is tempting to get lots of the novelty toys in the pet shop, but some of them can dangerous for pups when left to their own devices. I have seen a number of pups and adult dogs needing surgery to remove chewed up toys, and you really do not want to be doing that!

It won't take you long to work out what they will destroy quickly, or rip apart, so monitor any toys you think are not as tough - the best chews and toys for a Leavitt Bulldog are designed for strong breeds. Your little bulldog may look cute, but they are strong and love chewing.

My top chews and toys are as follows:

Kongs

They are brilliant, we will give you one in your pack but well worth getting a few, they come in different styles and sizes. Stuff them (by that I mean coat the inside) with a bit of cream cheese, pâté or a little bit or peanut butter. (Make sure the peanut butter is free from xylitol as its poisonous) While they are pricier than other options, most toys made by Kong, even their soft toys are pretty resilient - so you are in safe hand with them.

Another great tip with the kong is to mix up some peanut butter and water into a paste and pop the kong in the freezer - a great treat for a hot day. If you are out the house for a while, it keeps them busy for longer as it defrosts and is also good for teething mouths.

Antlers and horns

Go for the split ones if possible as they are slightly softer for the pups, they are are great for keeping them busy and not too smelly either which is bonus! Our guys love them and they last forever.

Vegetable based chews/Yak chews

There are a few type of vegetable - based chews (often in the shapes of hedgehogs and tooth brushes!) that are quite tough but your pup will be able to chew through as a little snack. I will give you some in your pack and I order a large box from Amazon. There is also a new Yak chew on the market which is made out of cheese! They are super tough and the dogs love them.

Wooden roots and Coffee wood

These are a firm favourite in our house - They are satisfyingly soft but still durable - The roots in particular are the puppies' favourite. Again not smelly or messy!

Mind games and interactive toys

These are toys that you don't necessarily leave your pup alone with, but are ideal for a rainy day to keep their minds busy and challenge them. They usually have a food - based reward involved and the dogs really enjoy them.

- The **Kong wobbler** is great
- **A snuffle mat**; A mat with lengths of fabric on it. You can hide treats in it, a calming and distracting game - anything nose/scent led is very positive and calming for your pup. Sniffing and foraging is a very mentally rewarding activity for your puppy.
- **Puzzle games** - these are plastic games that allow you to lift sections to hide treats in. The dog has to learn how to find the treats and they soon catch on. It's lots of fun to watch too. You can find them online more easily than in pet shops. Amazon is great as the reviews are handy to read through.

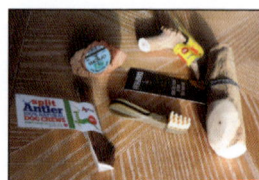

Fish skins

They do stink! But are great, healthy, low in fat and natural. The dogs love them so I have included them in your pack.

Tug toys

Teaching your puppy from the very start to play tug, beginning in a gentle and controlled way is an excellent idea. So investing in some 'tuggy', stretchy toys that you both play with is really useful. We have the tug toys put away, and only get them out during play time. It keeps them interested and gives a clear indication that tug is played only with certain toys.

Natural air dried meat or treats

I have provided you with some in your pack, but as a rule stick to treats with the highest meat content.

Things to avoid!

Anything easily ripped up and eaten!

If you want to get some novelty stuff, just keep an eye on them. Quality is better than quantity with toys. Some of the cheap toys are very flimsy and easily swallowed and destroyed. It is often better just to avoid them.

Treats with artificial colours, bulking agents, grains etc...

I have seen dogs so many times fed an excellent raw food diet, where the owners are doing everything right, but they then slip up and give treats such as Dentastix, Bakers bacon strips, Boneos, and so on. They are all terrible for your dog. Don't buy them, they will cause digestive issues, dehydrate them, cause hyperactivity- the list of negatives is endless.

Stick to natural healthy treats - the fewer ingredients, the better (always check the ingredients of anything you give your dog).

Nylabones

They are melted and reformed plastic, and the dogs will chew chunks off them They are bad for them to digest and not good for their health at all. So avoid!

Raw hide This is also not good for dogs, being salty and full of artificial chemicals. It is also actually a huge chocking hazard when it goes soft and there is a tendency for them to swallow it. Dogs and puppies also find it hard to cough it back up as it becomes slimy, and sticky.

Garden

I will have discussed your garden with you - if you don't already have a dog it is definitely worth checking around for any not so obvious escape areas. Although I have bred dogs for a number of years, I am yet to have a Leavitt Bulldog escape - tempting fate perhaps! But they are very much homebodies, so it is unusual for them to want to escape and roam.

It is worth mentioning too that our pups are expert gardeners - it might be worth moving any special pots out the way,! I have tried many times to have some nice plants and pots in the garden. If they are dug out and carried around the garden they end up squashed flat as plants make ideal beds!

There are also some plants and bushes that are poisonous to dogs so it worth having a double check you don't have any of these in your garden.

- Amaryllis bulbs
- Asparagus fern
- Azalea
- Cyclamen
- Daffodil bulbs
- Day lilies
- Delphiniums
- Foxgloves
- Hyacinth
- Hydrangea
- Ivy
- Laburnum
- Lily of the valley
- Lupins
- Morning glory
- Nightshade
- Rhododendron
- Rhubarb leaves
- Sweet pea
- Tulip bulbs
- Wisteria

POISONOUS PLANTS FOR DOGS
A Useful Guide

Rugs and mats

When we have a pup we do roll up the rugs! Once they have wee'd on the rug once it's a huge pain to stop them doing it again as the scent gets into the rugs and is hard to wash out. It's considering temporarily removing your rugs to help with housetraining.

Diet and Nutrition

It is no secret as to how a processed diet effects humans; eating too much fast and eating junk food, sugar and sweets, is going to have a negative effect on your health. It is no different with dogs - kibble, tinned food or any highly processed option is the dog equivalent to fast food and ready meals for humans. These options are over processed, lacking in nutrients, full of additives and are ultimately detrimental to your dog's health. We can all survive on a processed diet but the side effects on long term health are unquestionable, and it is exactly the same for our dogs. However, there is a great alternative to a 'traditional' processed diet for dogs: raw feeding, also known as B.A.R.F. (Biologically Appropriate Raw Food) This is based on a natural raw meat diet, and it's absolutely perfect diet for a dogs, being what their bodies are designed to eat. It may sound daunting, but I can assure you I have made it as simple as possible to get you started.

I will go through basics of raw feeding with you, addressing any concerns and busting some common myths surrounding raw feeding.

It is very easy to feel overwhelmed by the thought of feeding raw meat, but rest assured many of the owners I have dealt with over the years feel the same initially. I can promise you all these owners are complete raw feeding converts now. Some have become quite the experts - once you see the benefits and how much your dog loves raw food it's hard not become enthusiastic too!

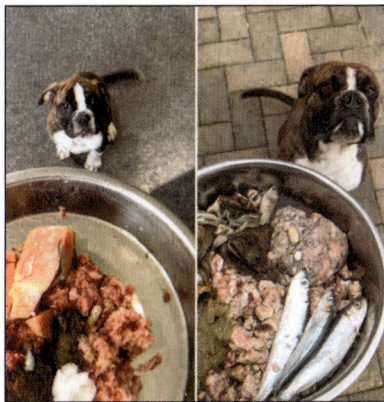

We have spent many years investing in every aspect of our breeding programme, trying to do everything in our power to ensure the dogs we breed are the healthiest possible.

One of the biggest factors in their good health and vitality is their diet.We have been feeding raw for the last 10 years and have seen such brilliant results with the dogs.

You have come this far in finding a dog that has been bred 'outside the box' with health as a priority, so why not continue these efforts through diet and nutrition?

We do understand that this is not always possible, and you may prefer to eventually change to a kibble, but we can't stress enough how important the correct diet is. So we will give a more extensive and specific guide to how to change over should you want to, as it can really upset your pup's tummy if you move to processed food too quickly. This can have other knock on effects on house training etc that could set you back. If you contact me I will help you get it right.

Raw feeding gets some bad press but it is becoming more commonly accepted; as with anything different to the norm, there are people getting it extremely wrong. This is not a case of feeding some raw beef mince from the supermarket, or chucking them some lamb shops. The raw diet you are feeding needs to be carefully and correctly balanced for your dog to thrive, and by that I mean it has to contain the correct percentage of meat, bone and offal. Do not panic if this sounds confusing because there are some excellent pre - balanced complete mince meat options that I use for young dogs, and this is what I have raised your puppy on. These minces take all the complications and guess work out of raw feeding and are 'ready to go' meals - you simply pull it out of the freezer, defrost the mince, put it in bowl and feed.

I follow a 80:10:10 guide.

This means that the diet is split into:

80% meat 10% bone and 10% offal

How much to feed?

We will send your pup home with enough food for a week and recommend you get stocked up before hand. I will put you in touch with the local expert supplier that we use ourselves. They have a great team who will advise you if needed, and they stock a variety of different brands of complete raw minces and great natural treats. They also deliver nationwide and have great customer service. (A good 2nd freezer will come in handy. We got ours from gumtree or eBay and they are perfect for filling up with pet food.)

At present (10 weeks old) each pup is getting approximately *300 - 350 g per day spread across 3 meals.* I also add 1or 2 sprats, a chicken wing or fish chunks in their lunch meal. My advice is to stick with that for now, they are all doing well on that amount. Please bear in mind I am feeding a whole litter so it may vary once you get your pup home and they are settled and less competitive with their litter mates.

They need approximately 5-6% of their body weight per day, spread across 3 meals.

Please don't worry if it doesn't look a lot compared to a kibble based diet, it is more than enough and is very nutritious. Think quality over quantity.

Your pup is about 6 - 7 kg (roughly)

- As your pup grows keep track of their weight and adjust accordingly
- At 12 weeks you can reduce the meals down to 2 feeds a day
- At 6 months you can feed once a day if you prefer - But some like to feed keep it twice - whatever you prefer.
- Overfeeding is one of the most common reasons for tummy upsets in young pups - over stimulation of the intestines can cause huge upset.
- TREATS! `remember if you are training with your pup, treats are also food so try to find something light and not too filling - boiled chicken is great!

Trust your eye - this is the best advice `I can give you!

Look at your dog daily and you will be able to see if you are feeding enough or too much – your pup should look light and athletic, with a clear tummy tuck. If they look too fat then slightly reduce the amount fed and vice versa - if they need to gain weight increase.

Don't worry too much if they always seem to be hungry or are not eating everything at once – all puppies go through stages that will effect their appetite.

Dogs that eat raw food often eat very fast too so don't panic.

Correct weight/body condition

A healthy dog should have a natural waist and you should be able to feel its ribcage. Puppies are supposed to be lean! The term 'puppy fat' is applied to pups who are still being nursed by their mothers. When a puppy arrives in its new home, it should start to loose this 'puppy fat' and gain shape and definition. You should be able to see a waist and this should happen within a few weeks of arrival in their new home.

One of the most detrimental things you can do for your puppy is over feed them. Food is not love - their joints will suffer, they will struggle and you will create other health issues if you allow the dog to carry too much weight. Please be careful. The guide below is very helpful to get an idea of the condition of your pup.

Feeding extras

Once owners find their feet with the raw feeding approach they will often begin to add in extra raw treats - now you can reduce the evening meal of meat occasionally and add 2 chicken wings or whole sprats, chunks of meat, or other soft bones like chicken/duck necks - these are all available from the raw food suppler, just ask her about good bones for pups.

Feeding bones

I know feeding bones like this maybe scary! It goes against everything we are told about dogs and bones being dangerous. But as long as the bones are raw they are soft and fully digestible and very enjoyable for the dogs to chew - I call the wings great toothbrushes for my dogs! Ruby is 10 now and has perfectly white healthy teeth and gums from regular bones. It is when a bone is cooked that it becomes dangerous, because the bone will splinter and can not be digested. This is extremely dangerous. Raw bones, however, are complete safe.

A word of warning though!

They will swallow them whole! I always feed bones outside, as dogs do like to make a mess, often spitting them out again after chewing to swallow back down. It can be quite a shock first time seeing them eat bones but do not worry as it's totally normal.

Supplements

Steve will have probably told you that he calls me "the dog witch!' because each one of the dogs has a different combination supplements added to their daily diet.

As a dog develops and matures there are some simple things to add to their diets that can help them thrive. I could fill pages with this subject but I will keep it simple and break it down to a couple of the essential supplements that I recommend adding to your dogs diet should you want to.

Ultimately the raw diet you are feeding is perfectly balanced so you don't really need to add anything in particular to keep your pup healthy. But there are some things that can help make them SUPER healthy!

A good quality oil A good oil added to their diet is a great idea. It helps brain development, joints, skin and overall health.

There are few options available: coconut oil, salmon oil, flax oil. A number of dog food companies have blended the best oils to create all round options too.

The key points is to try to ensure it is **cold pressed oil** - this ensures it's still complete and has all the goodness preserved. If you can get organic that's even better (particularly with coconut oil). aWhen storing it, keep it out of sunlight.

Dorwest Herbs do a great all round oil - Omega Star oil

Proflax are a company who specifically create dietary oil for dogs.

Holland and Barrett often do great offers on coconut oil.

Ester C

This is quite a complex subject and so is the explanation as to why I feed this to the dogs - but I will try to simplify it as best I can.

Dogs can not produce their own Vitamin C very well so when they run into something that may impose on their Vitamin C store (illness, vaccinations, infection, antibiotics or a diet lacking in nutrition) they will be lacking in Vitamin C.

This is not a hugely detrimental problem in itself, but there are side effects for a dog lacking in Vitamin C , particularly for a young, growing dog: Collagen production is controlled by Vitamin C levels, and collagen production is what keeps a dog's ligaments and tendons healthy, flexible and strong. A drop in Vitamin C levels will create a drop in collagen production and turn put ligament health at risk. This is a problem in young, powerful and agile breeds like ours. The end result can be issues with ligaments, with the worst case scenario being ligament ruptures in knees and other joint issues.

This is why I religiously supplement all my dogs, including pregnant mothers and puppies with Vitamin C - more specifically Ester C, as this is the most digestible version for dogs.

I also give them a double dose 3 days before and 4 days after a course of vaccinations and throughout any form of antibiotic use.

Training Advice

To cover training in this guide is quite ambitious of me, as it is never ending and I am still learning continuously. I have already explained I am no dog trainer; I can offer you my advice and opinion based only on my experience of living with 9+ Leavitt Bulldogs, raising them from pups over the last 12 years, along with supporting their families on a daily basis. I am going to try and go through some of the basics with you to get you started.

The 'Puppy Culture' programme gets you and your pup off to a great start, giving you a clear guide to follow which can be used as the pup matures and develops. However it won't help you with everything forever unfortunately and ultimately the success and happiness of your pup is very much in your hands going forward.

Find a trainer

Many years ago when I first had dogs I would have never dreamed of going to a dog trainer. It seemed unnecessary and expensive, to be perfectly honest. Now, I go to puppy training class with every puppy I have. It is not about experience, or knowledge - I like to go to trainer to keep me on my toes and ensure I have a structured approach. I see it as a great investment in a puppy that will be our companion for the next decade.

To get started, the first step is finding a trainer that you like, someone that you and your dog can build a relationship with and that you can call on as and when you need them.

When you are looking at trainers it is a good idea to go along and watch their puppy class, observing how they interact with the dogs and owners. Go for someone you click with, being impressed with their abilities is important, but you want to feel comfortable with them too. If you are relaxed, so is the dog.

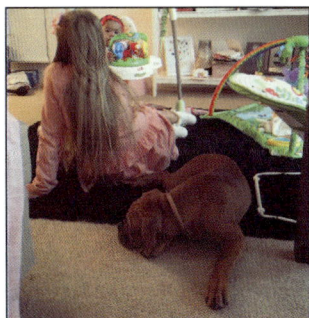

A trainer that is experienced with bull breeds is important - they are different to other breeds, although many will argue they are not. I spend enough time around all different breeds and there is no question bull breeds (in particular Leavitt Bulldogs) require an experienced trainer. Taking your time to finding the right trainer is really beneficial.

There are lots of terrible dog trainers out there. If you need help finding a trainer near you, I will help you.

Dog training is broken down into different methods, and it is actually quite complex, controversial and quite a minefield once you start looking into it. Hopefully this explanation will help you to identify what you are looking for and what type of training you want you follow with your puppy.

Most trainers will follow a certain method or approach.

A simple way to explain the varieties is by looking at the method in which the dog is trained/motivated/disciplined. This very basically falls into 3 main categories:

Postive:

This is reward based training, allowing the dog to think for itself in a relaxed way where you are rewarding them positively when they act correctly, and ignoring the bad behaviour. This is also known as force free training, or purely positive training. It's a stress free approach (for the dog) and certainly a more modern way of handling dogs. You will be familiar with it through 'Puppy Culture' as this is foundation of the 'Puppy Culture' method. It's great way for young puppies to build confidence and to bond with their families. These methods often encourage the use of harnesses over collars and lots of food - based luring and distraction.

Alpha/Dominance:

This training approach is a very firm, controlled and a dominant approach, based on the idea that dogs are pack animals and need a leader to live a happy life and behave. The approach is very direct, often forcing behaviour and firmly correcting the dog, as opposed to guiding them to make the right choice. Punishment is used to discourage unwanted behaviour. This is a quite an old fashioned approach to training, and although it is often used with bull breeds it doesn't always have the desired long term effect of creating a happy dog. You will often see the use of choke chains, prong collars and other equipment to control a dog.

Balanced:

This is the middle ground between the two. A balanced approach is what it says on the tin: a balance of the methods above.

Positive reinforcement when needed, alongside negative punishment. However the negative punishment is never pain or aggression; instead it will be more of a verbal correction, startle or touch if the dog is in a heightened state.

They use a combination of harnesses and Collars or e - collars in older dogs as well as treats and toys.

The aim is to raise a a respectful dog that understands the boundaries but is happy and relaxed.

I have mentioned these three methods as they are the most common types you will come across when choosing a trainer. There are other sub categories, but I wanted to narrow it down and keep it simple.

Leavitt Bulldogs are not your average dog, they require a high level of training to be the best they can be, and in my experience respond well to a balanced and structured approach to training. When it comes to training my own dogs I have had good results with positive training, particularly with young pups. I also enforce a balanced approach, with clear and direct negative correction if ever needed in the form of verbal correction and use of body language. I am not supportive of methods that dominate or act aggressively towards dogs - they are counterproductive and unnecessary and, in the long term, create more problems.

When raising a puppy myself I am very clear with them about what is unacceptable, I keep it black and white for them. I encourage the behaviour I want from them, using a clicker and focus on a positive and happy relationship with my pups.

I also learn a lot from watching the older dogs; if a young pup is out of line, for instance biting too hard, becoming over excited or boisterous, then the older dogs will reprimand the pup. This is never in an aggressive way, but in a calm, clear,

direct and controlled manner This is the approach I adopt when setting boundaries with the puppies.

My Training Tips:

1 *Make a plan:*

As a family, sit down and discuss your approach - you MUST be reading from the same page, every single family member. No matter how young the youngest human is, or how much of a teenager you have, it is imperative you are doing the same things. Consistency is key, if the dog spots a weakness in your family unit it can make for some unwanted behaviour.

Set your rules together - No sofa must mean no sofa. If one person lets them on, everyone else will have a hard time reinforcing the rules agreed by everyone.

The dog is the family's responsibility as a unit. So work together.

- Use the same commands.
- Stick to the same routine.
- Agree on the rules and stick to them.

2.- *The Garden first!*

It is tempting to get your pup home and take them indoors and play and make a fuss of them but this is not the best idea! My advice is ... **head to the garden first.**

Take them outside (with your treats ready in your hand) and wait, silently. Don't talk to them as it will distract them, just watch and wait until they have a wee or a poo. They may be a bit fretful or just be off exploring, but they will go to the toilet eventually, especially after a long car journey. When they do go timing is KEY!
As they begin, calmly praise them and as they are about to finish give them a treat. Don't worry if they are still having a wee as you treat them, that's fine. Good in fact, as then they will know for sure what they are doing is correct.

Once this has been done they will know where the correct place is to go to the toilet, or at least have an idea.
That's the start of house training and you can now take them in and have a little play and a cuddle!!

3- *Brief visitors beforehand:*

Do not let visitors come over just to meet the pup if they are going to be excitable. Exciting as a new puppy is, you are setting the foundations now for how you want your pup to behave towards visitors as a 25kg adult!

Ensure that you do not let the pup interact with visitors until they are calm - both visitors and dog!

When the dog relaxes, reward it and and give it a treat. Encourage gentle and calm behaviour and swiftly correct the bad ie biting and jumping up.

3. *Consistency:*

I can not stress enough the importance of this, get set up, create a routine and stick to it. Dogs thrive with routine as a pup and it will set them up for success. Take them to the same toilet spot, keep the same routine as dinner is served, feed them the same way and it will only take days for them to pick up your routine.

4. *Keep a pocket full treats or a pot on the side:*

Try to avoid missing an opportunity to treat, I have full pockets of dog treats always. There is nothing worse than missing a perfect wee in the garden!

5. *Timing:*

Correct timing is essential when using positive reinforcement.

The reward must occur immediately—within seconds—or your pet may not associate it with the proper action.

For example, if you have your dog sit but reward him after he's stood back up, he'll think he's being rewarded for standing up.

Using a clicker to mark the correct behaviour can improve your timing and also help your dog understand the connection between the correct behaviour and the treat.

5. *Anticipate your puppy, watch them closely:*

Get to learn their **body language** - it helps you anticipate behaviours and gives you great power when it comes to training: If they have had a nap, take them out to the garden as soon as they wake up. They always wee after a nap!

If the pup is nipping, this is a sign it is over tired, so call it a day and let them rest.

7. *Take them everywhere:*

Even without the vaccinations you can carry them to places. The more they see and experience the better rounded they will become, so let people meet them and stroke them (calmly).
I always take treats for young children to give the pup when it is sitting nicely to encourage calm behaviour.

"OUT"

Teach the 'OUT" command - it is highly a highly valuable skill that is the pathway to all games, and opens up your ability to teach impulse control, a very very important skill for a Leavitt Bulldog. You can do this simply by saying the word and swiping the toy for a treat, repeating it over and over and you can slowly faze out the treat as continuation of the game it becomes the reward.

If you are playing tug, make it clear that following the "out" the dog sits and make eye contact before the game continues. You must reinforce that they need to be controlled to play with you.

Play!

Do not underestimate the power of play, it is a brilliant way to bond with your pup, but keep it controlled and structured. Once you have mastered "out" you can play Tug, its a hugely rewarding game for a dog, and a great game to introduce on walks to keep them focused on you. It makes you very interesting!

"Fetch" is also a great game to encourage, you can do this by swapping balls thrown at first, building up the distance. We have owners playing frisbee and interactive scent games too. There are lots of things to do with your pup.

Recall

Recall is one the most important, if not the most important skills, to teach your dog. It needs to be done from day one: at home, indoors in a controlled environment ,with no distractions. Practice repeat, repeat, repeat over and over again until you think you can't do it anymore!

The key point to a successful recall is take tiny little steps. This can not be rushed and the process needs to built up very slowly.

You can use your voice, a whistle, or a certain call but what you must ensure is that it is used consistently every time and, most importantly, is followed by a treat.

Call/whistle … treat ….call/whistle…treat….

What you are creating here is called a conditioned response in your puppy's brain: A response to the sound to make them want to come to you for a treat.

Build up to doing this when they are napping, when they turn away, are in another room, or in the garden. Make it the best, most fun and exciting game.

One of my tips for recall is not to 'poison' your call. By that I mean; set them (and you) up success in the early stages - keep it simple and make it work every time. If the dog has lost focus, seen something and started running then give one or two attempts, but don't try and recall repeatedly, as it is unlikely it will work, you will get frustrated and lose faith. You want the call to be a success every time, to outweigh the occasional failure.

Coupled with the recall, once the dog has returned give lots of treats, play, fuss and praise. They will soon realise coming back to you is BRILLIANT!

Meeting other dogs/Puppy clubs etc

I wanted to do a separate section for this subject as it is a huge factor in the raising of our pups. It is an issue I run into time and time again with every litter.

Meeting other dogs is inevitable - when you are the park, on the street or just day to day living. I can not stress the importance of your role in this part of your dog's life:

You are your dog's voice and their protector, so avoid at all costs running into a strange dog that can have a negative effect on their development. By that I mean a badly behaved dog, one that is overbearing, rude, dominate or aggressive. Do not be afraid to tell other owners to keep their dog away, it can just take one of two bad experiences to really create problems that can stay with a young pup for a lifetime.

I don't believe dogs need friends at the park. They don't have to meet every dog they see and they need protection from badly behaved and antisocial dogs.

Playing and interacting with balanced, calm and trustworthy older dogs is great, but you still need to ensure you are in control and can call your pup away when needed.

Be the centre of their world!

My approach to successfully passing other dogs out walking is to ensure I am the centre of my pups world: I want them to see another dog and automatically make eye contact with me, not pulling on the lead to 'say hello'. 'Saying Hello' to other dogs is not a behaviour you want to encourage, as when you have a fully grown adult Leavitt Bulldog, many dogs do not want to say hello. You dogs does not need friends at the park in the early stages of bonding with you on a walk- you are your dog's best friend. You want be the most import being on the planet.

This is achievable if you are really interactive on dog walks: as I mentioned above, stopping to play a game of Tug, keeping a certain toy just for dog walks is a great idea - this makes it high value toy and very interesting to them. Always keep stocked up on extra tasty treats (boiled chicken or cheese saved just for high focus times works great).

If you just click on the lead and walk along the road to the park: being uninteresting and boring , can you blame your dog for charging off the moment they see another dog? You are not exciting to them, they are getting no thrill or enjoyment from you. But the dog across the other side of the road or park is VERY exciting. The moment you become boring you have lost! So stay fun, positive and keep a happy 'energy' and you will keep their focus.

Do not be afraid to tell other owners that your pup is in training and not ready to meet other dogs. It will pay off the long run. As I said, you are your dog's voice, so be confident when speaking up for them.

Puppy Clubs free play etc:

This type of puppy socialising is normally set up by vets or day care centres. My personal advice is to avoid these kind of set ups. They are a recipe for disaster as they are often a free for all with very little professional guidance in place. All your pup learns is heightened and uncontrollable play which is not structured and encourages bad habits.

Responsible adults:

Finding a calm, responsible older dog is a brilliant idea! They will be a 'friend' for your pup. They will learn important and valuable lessons from them which will help their social development hugely! Make sure the older dog has an escape route though! You don't want an annoying pup driving them mad, so watch closely.

House training

The key to successful house training is staying ahead and creating a routine.

On average, most pups will poo around about 10- 20 mins after eating.
They will wee almost every time they wake up from a nap!
My advice is don't feed later than 5 at night at the very latest.
The earlier you let them out in the morning the better, because if they hear you upstairs or get woken up then the chances are they will wake up and need to go instantly. So to avoid an accident let them out right away before anything else.

How long can a puppy hold it's bladder?

How long a puppy can actually hold her bladder depends on the puppy's age. In theory, a pup is able to hold their bladder for roughly one hour per month of their age. I said "in theory" as, in my experience, a puppy needs to "go" a lot more often than once every 2 hours at 8 weeks old.
Below is a table that shows how long puppies can hold their bladder based on age:

Age	Time can hold
8 weeks	2 hours
12 weeks	3hours
16 weeks	4 hours

I would use the age guide as the maximum time puppies are able to hold their bladder if they are confined to a crate. If you had your pup in a crate then they would likely be able to hold their bladder for this length of time.
However, if your pup is loose in the house with you, then I'd suggest that you'll need to take her outside more frequently. For example, it would be closer to every 30-40

minutes at 8 weeks old. Definitely at least every hour. As they get older, you'll be able to decrease the frequency and you should soon start to notice a pattern which will be your puppy's schedule. Bear in mind , if the weather is hot then they are likely to be drinking a lot more water and will need to go out more often too.

I also take up water from the pen at night. Raw fed dogs do not drink lots anyway, and there is no need to have them drinking all night. It will make house training much easier in the early stages.

Training equipment

1. Y shaped harness - a good harness is great for a young pup as it gives them support and freedom to build confidence and explore. But it's important it is a Y shaped harness that does not restrict shoulder movement. Halti make great ones, as do a company called Perfect Fit.
2. Good flat collar and double click training lead - these are leads with clips on both ends so you can shorten or extend the length. Again, Halti do excellent ones (from Pets at Home or Amazon)
3. Treat bag - A treat bag saves your coat pockets from being full of stinky treats! Find one that is easy to use with one hand and allows you to access the treats quickly.
4. Long line - this is a very long lead, they are handy to have ready. They are very important and help when working on recall. Use it to build up distance as recall becomes more reliable.
5. High value toys - these are toys that are not played with everyday - really special ones that they are excited by which are put away when being used for training.
6. High value treats - these are really tasty - fArthur he will jump through fire for cut-up tinned hotdogs! I don't feed him many, but when they are out I can be sure I have his full attention, For Ruby it's Cheese! They all have a favourite, so keep it in reserve for super high focus tasks.

To summarise: work at keeping training short, exciting and really fun. Just a few minutes a day is enough. You may not feel like it, but it will be 'going in' I promise you, although there will be days when you think you are wasting your time. Then it will suddenly click and you will think they are a canine genius! If you are having a bad day and feeling frustrated, stop and start again another day.

Being positive and giving lots of rewards is great, but you also need to be firm and clear when it comes to boundaries. These are big strong, smart and complex dogs at times.

Be very clear of their place in your family and what is expected from them. Keep it black and white or right and wrong and they will settle nicely.

You will have hard days, and you will feel like they are going backwards. So know when to stop, walk away and start fresh the next day.

Fear Periods

Fear periods are developmental stages where a puppy will suddenly become unsure, reluctant or scared of situations or objects they have normally been fine with. They are a normal part of development, and I have yet to meet a pup that hasn't experienced a fear period of some form, sometimes they are short and hardly noticeable and other times they can be quite significant. The most important thing to remember is do not panic, or become too disheartened, it's normal and as long as you support your pup and deal with it calmly, they will be absolutely fine.

The first fear period happens here with me, around 8 - 10 weeks old (hence why I keep them here until 10 weeks). I have become good at spotting this early one and can work them through it without too much hassle.
The second one will happen will happen when they are with you, but like I said above: you may not even notice it with some pups, whereas with others it will be very obvious.

This second fear period happens around 6 - 12 months of age (depending on the maturity of your pup). This is a large range as they can drop in and out of fear periods through out this time.

This fear period is believed to be tied to your dog's hormones and growth spurts. So often large breeds experience this later on in their development compared to a smaller breeds.

In the wild, maturing pups are allowed to go on hunts with the rest of the pack. But it is important for them to learn to stick with the pack for safety, as they are not yet mature enough to cope with many experiences alone. It is their instinct at this age to run from things that are unfamiliar or new, and this fearful period is actually important in keeping them safe and preparing them for maturity.

Your pup may seem overly fretful, defensive or even become protective or more territorial. Owners often report the fear seems to come out of the blue, which can seem confusing and disheartening but don't panic. They do settle as long as you are consistent, calm and help work them through things.

How to move your puppy through something scary!

If your puppy gets spooked by something or seems unusually timid in a situation, don't worry. It is important to be gently reassuring. Although there is an old fashioned view that if you try to calm a scared dog you will encourage them to be scared, this is not strictly true. However it is important to be aware that being calming and reassuring is very different to 'fussing'. The important part of this process is making sure you are calm, relaxed and confident. Give them time, encourage them forward and move them forward through the situation, give lots of praise and introduce something they like! Something like a licky mat with peanut butter often works a treat to help make it positive.

Licking a naturally calming behaviour in dogs - it's a good tip to remember! If you can get your pup too lick something during a stressful experience you will get them to come out the other side with a positive experience. A tube of Primula cheese is a great tool for this, so take it to the vets, or alongside busy roads or other loud places where you feel they may need some positive association.

Do not 'flood' your pup if they are scared: by flood I mean do not force them or overload them with an experience they are already struggling with. It could be detrimental to their long term development, particularly during fear periods.

Remember to stay positive, keep it fun and if you have a bad day write it off and start fresh the next day.

Managing Dogs and Kids

Whilst we are all aware how wonderful these dogs are with kids, it is still crucially important that you manage the interaction between the children in the home and the dogs really carefully. Your puppy is used to children and will warm to them. But this is because they have been handled calmly and gently. This does not just apply to the puppies in our home, but to the adults too. I do not leave the dogs unattended with the children ever, and I am extremely strict with how the dogs behave around them. They are not allowed to jump up, nip, pull at clothing, chase feet or shoes and act in anyway that could be dangerous to the kids or themselves. Vice versa the children need to treat the dogs with the same respect.

It is very easy to be lured into a false sense of security with a well mannered dog.

But be aware even as adults they are still dogs: They can only react to any situation as a dog, and that can include snapping, growling, even biting if they are uncomfortable upset or hurt .

Never allow your child to climb on, pull at, man handle or sit on the dog, it is not cute funny or a testament to a good temperament. Read your dog carefully at all times around your children, there are times they don't want to be cuddled with arms around necks and body. You have no way of knowing just how the dog is feeling, they could have an injury you can't see, a sore ear etc

If a dog is in their bed its their space, do not allow the children to get into the dogs bed with them, it is not fair and they need their own space and time away from us humans too.

Get your children involved with training, get them a certain special toy they play together with, they can watch training videos on YouTube and practice, they can create puzzles, get simple agility equipment and really bone with the dogs. These are all positive ways your kids can get close to the dog and that the dog really appreciates and enjoys.

Exercise

I have given you a brilliant exercise book written by the creators of 'Puppy Culture' - this covers majority of what you need to know. I have also included some further advice I have learned over the years, and how we raise our young dogs.

Exercise is a very important part of your pup's upbringing - if done properly it can help with training, bonding and also keep your pup stimulated and healthy. However it is very easy to **OVER EXERCISE** a young growing dog, which can lead to serious injury and joint issues later in life, so little and often is great to start off with.

It is important to keep exercise gentle and fun, with lots of toys and gentle games like fetch. Going through basic obedience and playing games is as equally as beneficial as a walk around the block. Mental exercise will do wonders in tiring out a young pup.

There is no definitive answer as to how much exercise each pup needs, or how much can create problems. However I can offer you some sensible guidelines. With the health screening in our dogs we are hoping that your puppy has sound, genetically strong joints passed from its parents, and is not horribly overweight, so in all honesty, it can take really quite a LOT of exercise without serious damage. Taking into consideration that both your pup's parents and ancestors have been screened and tested for joint disease, having hips and elbows scored (both good scores too!) we are hoping the they have a very good chance of having genetically strong joints. However, this is not guaranteed. There is also an environmental factor that comes into play with joint health.

As a rule, healthy joints are harder to damage than weak ones.

That being said, no matter how much we have done to attempt to breed dogs with a higher chance of healthy, strong joints, common sense is still needed. The best way to think of it that your pup is a baby, and babies need to be taken care of because they cannot make rational decisions for themselves. Pups like small children, run on adrenaline, especially during new and exciting experiences, and do not know 'when to stop'. So YOU need to make that decision for them. As a young dog hits exhaustion point during exercise, damage can then start to occur pretty easily. Your puppy will not acknowledge he has hit exhaustion point. From his behaviour he may seem FULL of beans and up for it, especially if interacting with other dogs.

I have seen many good dogs in a bad way from over exercising as a youngster;

It is crucial that I make it clear that over exercising, combined with over feeding are the most detrimental factors in a dog's upbringing. So please take this and the 'Puppy Culture' book on board - this advice is absolutely crucial for the long term health of your dog.

Jumping

Please avoid letting your pup jump off things like sofas and chairs, particularly onto slippery, hard wooden flooring or tiles. I try and follow the rule with my youngsters of all 4 feet on the ground until they are 12 months old.

Swimming

Swimming is without a doubt the absolute best exercise your pup can get. I highly recommend getting them used to water; you can go a hydrotherapy class if possible or take them to a lake or beach. There are some great doggy lifejackets that will help build their confidence whilst learning to swim.

Cupboard Essentials

There are a few really useful products that I recommend all owners to have on hand with a dog ; owning them can help you avoid a costly vet's trip for routine issues. I can promise you that living with my lot means I have come across quite an array of conditions, all of them fixable with these items. It goes without saying that if something serious happens, the vets are needed. But for minor cuts, grazes, rashes and bumps theses products can often help!

1. **Pro Kolin** You can buy this from Amazon or Pets at Home. It comes in a plastic syringe. It is a probiotic paste that is designed to settle their tummies if they are suffering from diarrhoea. It is fantastic and is my first port of call if we have any 'runny tummies.'

2. **Tree Barks Powder** You can buy this from Dorwest Herbs. It is quite similar to Pro Kolin and helps bring down tummy inflammation and firm up stools. It can be fed along with food over a longer period than Pro Kolin to help stabilise an upset tummy and support the digestive system.

3. **Piriton** This is an essential for me, particularly during the summer in case the dogs get stung by a wasp or bee. It can also be used to treat any form of reaction to grass or pesticide etc. This is not for long term use, more for an instant relief and I only ever have to give it for a few days to calm the reaction down. If it is still needed after 2/3 days, a vet's trip is in order.

4. **Leucillin** Antiseptic Skin Care Spray - available from Amazon, this is a super all round antiseptic skin spray for minor cuts and grazes.
5. Camomile tea bags - organic bags are best, and are great to brew and let cool to use on 'sticky' eyes, which my guys will occasionally get if they have been running in long grass. Using these for a few days clears it up perfectly.
6. **Hibiscrub** This is a great skin cleaner, great for rinsing a dog off and washing paws etc, and can also be used for cleaning small cuts and grazes.

Collection Day

It is always hard to see the pups we have loved so much over the last 10 weeks leave our home, but knowing they are coming to your family makes it all worth while.

You may want to hold them in the car or put them in a crate: that is up to you. It is nice to bond and have a cuddle, but they will be used to traveling in the crate with the blanket I give you and a chew, particularly for longer journeys. It is wise to decide how you like them to travel with you before hand.

I will have taken them out in the car individually over the last few weeks so hopefully it won't be too stressful for them. My aim is to get them used to traveling in the car to avoid motion sickness and to make their journey to your home as relaxing as possible for all of you!

Your pup is insured for 4 weeks, and I will give you the relevant paper work. It will be just a case of continuing the plan or having a shop around for the best price and policy. You could also speak to existing owners - I can put you in touch with them.

Your pup will have had their first vaccination at 7-8 weeks along with being microchipped. The paperwork will have already been transferred into your name and will be in your folder along with the insurance and other paperwork.

If possible, I will have got you to collect your puppy as early in the day as you can, this gives them the afternoon to settle at your home and familiarise themselves with their new surroundings. If you have an existing dog, it's always wise for the two to meet in the day time and settle down for the evening together. I will not have fed them if its early as they always travel better without a full belly. I will have also given you a defrosted meal ready for you to give when they get settled at home.

First few days at home

It will take everyone a few days to find their feet!

My advice is to keep things nice and calm, but please do not worry about wrapping them up in cotton wool. It is a busy home here, they are used to lots going on, so don't alter your lifestyle too much.

The priority is making the most of the last 2 weeks of the puppy culture so get stuck into training and socialising. Keep it short and fun, bond with them, love them and play with them.

I always mention that is not uncommon for your pup to have a bit of runny tummy in the first few days, not always, but it has happened occasionally. Please do not panic, it's normally due to the excitement and changes, and will settle down. I have given you some Tree Barks powder, so add a teaspoon across the 3 meals for a few days and it will help firm up the puppies stool quickly.

You may want to book a visit to the vet too just to to have your puppy checked over and book in their second vaccination.

The first night for each pup can really vary, I still have not worked out any rhyme or reason to how they will behave. Sometimes the noisier pups here settled without a peep, and the calmer quieter pups howl the house down, there is just no telling!

It is impossible to prepare them completely for a whole new home, but there are some things we can do to help them settle well, such as giving them familiar bedding, or having a radio on quietly (I play classical here as its great back ground noise).

If they do cry and bark what you do is really up to you, but with my own pups I leave them to settle alone with a chew. They will soon realise that barking like crazy will not get them anywhere. What you must be aware of is that what you do now will set the rules in their minds as to what happens when they bark and cry - if their actions get a reaction and attention from you they will continue doing it. So be careful how you engage with them when they are barking and whining. They will learn to settle eventually. They have all had time alone from the litter whilst they are here, not during the night, but throughout the day.

By this point you will be aware that I am here to support both you and your pup as much as is needed. I am here to offer advice when ever possible, and if can not help I will find someone that can. I see everyone that has a pup from me as part of our extended family.

I look forward to watching your pup grow and thrive with you, and will be grateful to be updated as much as you want.

There is nothing more rewarding than seeing a pup that was born into my hands grow up and become a loved family member.
That's been the plan all along, and why I do everything I do to share these wonderful dogs.

Printed in Great Britain
by Amazon

83126700R00022